So We're Growing Older

John E. Biegert

WIPF & STOCK · Eugene, Oregon

Wipf and Stock Publishers
199 W 8th Ave, Suite 3
Eugene, OR 97401

So We're Growing Older
By Biegert, John E.

ISBN 13: 978-1-60608-216-4
Publication date 10/13/2008
Previously published by Pilgrim Press, 1982

Preface

I am growing older. You are growing older. And as we look around us, we know that we are not alone. This becomes even more apparent when we consider that in 1900 only 4 percent of the population of the United States were over age 65. In 1980 more than 11 percent were 65 or older, and by the year 2035 those over 65 will have reached between 18 and 23 percent of the total.

Some of us grow older gracefully; some of us, not so gracefully. For some of us, aging is a problem, even though we dislike the alternative. I hope the thoughts, poems, prayers, and selections from the scriptures contained in the pages that follow will benefit all of us who are growing older!

Why Focus on the Subject?

It is important that we reflect on growing older because next to dying the recognition that we are aging is the most profound shock of our lifetime. As the years go by we are confronted by two situations that can become for us major crises.

For one, we are called upon to adjust to a decline in physical vigor and a change in our physical characteristics. Watching baseball on television is more inviting than going to the ball park. Cooking dinner becomes a chore. A golf cart looks more and more attractive than a caddy. Tennis doubles become much more appealing than singles. We chuckle with empathy when a child asks an adult with thinning hair, "Why do you let your face grow so high?" We find ourselves with above average interest reading Ann Landers' reply to the lady who inquired whether or not a face-lift would make her feel better about herself when she views her image in a mirror.

But, in addition to physical changes, there are other changes with which we are confronted that can become for us major crises. Children reach the age when they depart from home for school or work. Instead of being only parents we also become grandparents. The death of parents and spouse often must be faced.

The questions thus become: How do we cope with growing older? What qualities do we need to insure that the foregoing happenings become just events and not crises? It is my conclusion that there are six qualities, in particular, that we must incorporate into our being if we are successfully to cope with growing older.

Possess a Right Attitude

Essential to coping with growing older in a successful manner is, first of all, *the possession of a right attitude.* All of us have heard the maxim that one is as old as one feels. And the important truth therein is that so much of life is a matter of mind. Although much that is connected with our physical being cannot easily be changed, we can change our mind, that is, our way of thinking and feeling about our present state in life.

This is to say that we must be willing to accept the fact that if we live we are going to grow old. Ponce de Leon found no "fountain of youth," nor can we expect to find one, contrary to what much contemporary advertising would have us believe. The already-mentioned physiological and sociological changes most likely will occur. But instead of saying in resignation, "I'm done in; I'm over the hill," a person possessing the right attitude for coping with growing older will affirm, "Today is the first day of the rest of my life." And he or she will ask the vital question, "What are the constructive ways of growing older and staying alive as long as I live?"

Essa Lott still had such a right attitude when she was ninety years old and wrote "So We're Growing Older":

> It is just one's state of mind.
> We do not grow older by living
> a number of years. We grow old by
> deserting our ideals and our
> will to accomplish.

Years may grey our hair and
wrinkle our skin, but to give
up Faith wrinkles our soul.

We are as young as our Faith
and as old as our fears.

Let's think of others, and
instead of indulging in self-pity
try to lend a helping hand to
someone less fortunate than we.*

Be Flexible

To ask how we can truly live as long as life is ours suggests a second quality essential for coping with growing older—*flexibility* as opposed to rigidity. The longer we live the easier it is to become set in our ways, to fall into ruts, to become stagnant, to be deceived by the often-cited but grossly untrue statement, "I can't change." In most facets of life this is untrue, for "I can't change," when translated honestly means, "I don't want to change!"

The field of psychology suggests that two types of flexibility are needed. Mental flexibility is necessary—the ability to be open to new ideas, the willingness to recognize that we do not possess all life's final and correct answers. Then, too, we need the capacity to invest strong emotions in *new* relationships and activities. How poor is the person who enjoys at forty, fifty, or sixty only those activities that he or she enjoyed at twenty or whose close friends are only those from high school or college days. For the essence of Bruce Barton's statement is quite true, "When you're through changing, you're through."

---

*Used by permission of Paul Rodgers.

Develop a Variety of Interests

The third quality essential for growing older gracefully can be labeled *ego differentiation.* By this is meant the capacity to pursue and enjoy a varied set of activities in life and the capacity to value oneself for a variety of reasons. Or, to express this concept in common language, ego differentiation is a person's ability not to put all of his or her eggs into one basket!

Parents, in particular, talk a great deal about desiring that their children develop well-rounded personalities, that they lead well-rounded lives, that they learn to share in and enjoy a wide variety of experiences. However, we sometimes forget that what is good for children is just as essential for us. In fact, it becomes increasingly so the older we grow.

How sad it is when a couple has no common interests or enjoyments other than their children! This is why so many twenty- and thirty-year marriages go on the rocks and fall apart. And how tragic when a man or woman is, for all practical purposes, married to his or her job and continually eats, drinks, and sleeps it! What little hope there is for a happy and gratifying retirement.

We Are More than Our Bodies

A fourth quality that we who are growing older would do well to cultivate is *body transcendence and satisfaction.* The unnamed preacher who authored the book of Ecclesiastes wrote about "the day when the keepers of the house [the arms and hands] tremble, and the strong men [the legs] are bent, and the grinders [the teeth] cease because they are few, and those that look through the windows [the eyes] are dimmed . . . [12:3]." None of us is so naive as to believe that this does not occur as the years go by.

Thus, rather than basing positive feelings about ourselves and being able to affirm, "I'm OK" solely on a physical basis, the one who is able to cope with growing older will have the capacity to feel whole and worthwhile because of one's social and mental activities, whether or not one's health is good. One will be able to accept and feel content with what he or she does have in respect to bodily prowess instead of just mourn for what is lacking. And instead of becoming mired in the pit of depression when confronted by the realization that one no longer has the body of a teenager, the person successfully coping with growing older will seek to match the ways of one's life to the capabilities of one's body.

This quality of body transcendence and satisfaction was well illustrated in the life of John Quincy Adams who, at the age of eighty, met a friend on a Boston street. "'Good morning,' said the friend, 'and how is John Quincy Adams today?' 'Thank you,' the ex-president replied, 'John Quincy Adams himself is well, quite well, I thank you. But the house in which he lives at present is becoming dilapidated. It is tottering upon its foundations. Time and the seasons have nearly destroyed it. Its roof is pretty well worn out. Its walls are much shattered and it trembles with every wind. The old tenement is becoming almost uninhabitable and I think John Quincy Adams will have to move out of it soon. But he himself is quite well, quite well.'" (Harry Emerson Fosdick, *The Meaning of Faith*, p. 68)

Moving Beyond Self

The fifth quality needed as we age is yet another kind of transcendence, *ego transcendence.* Wrote Paul Scherer: "It is never long before the life that has no meaning beyond its own narrow horizons begins to grow emptier and emptier. With no interest left but self-interest, there is soon no interest left. With Job it was disaster; with others routine, a listless boredom that plods down the hours watching the clock. . . ." (*Love Is a Spendthrift*, p. 66)

It was the renowned physician, theologian, and humanitarian Albert Schweitzer who suggested that the only ones among us who will be really happy are those who have sought and found how to serve. Furthermore, said Schweitzer: "What every individual has to contribute remains his own secret. But we must all mutually share in the knowledge that our existence only attains its true value when we have experienced in ourselves the truth of the declaration: 'He who loses his life shall find it.'" (*Civilization and Ethics*, p. 270)

Yes, finding satisfaction lies in fulfilling the needs of others and in having the capacity to engage in actions gratifying to them, similar to what Jesus once said about serving and ministering, focusing on others instead of always wanting to be the focal point ourselves!

A Meaningful Faith

The sixth and final suggestion for coping with growing older is to acquire or possess *a meaningful faith*. We need, on the one hand, a faith that assures us who live in this youth-oriented culture that it is not shameful to grow older. Unfortunately we, today, have lost the philosophy prevalent in biblical times. In the Talmud—an encyclopedia of Jewish tradition supplementing the scriptures—it is said that at forty a person has understanding, at fifty one gives counsel, and at eighty one has special strength. Life, from this perspective, moves toward a climax. And it is hopeful—recognizing that each chapter has its place and something to offer.

At the same time, we need the faith of the psalmist who testified in Psalm 71 to the strength and help God gave him in his youth and who knew that even as the years went by he never would be alone because God would be with him. Yes, the older we become the more we need to hear and take to heart the words of Helen Keller: "A simple childlike faith in a Divine Friend solves all the problems that come to us. . . . Difficulties meet us at every turn. They are the accompaniment of life. . . . The surest way to meet them is to assume that we are immortal and that we have a friend who 'slumbers not, nor sleeps,' and who watches over us and guides us—if we but let him." (*The Open Door,* p. 20)

Some Difficult Choices

Growing older often brings with it the need for us to make some difficult choices. Perhaps the two most difficult are: "When should I retire, and where shall I live?"

"When should I retire?" If this is not determined by our employer we must weigh the alternative either of continuing to maintain the schedule and pace that have been ours or choosing a life-style wherein our time and energies can be used more at our own discretion. Which path we follow might be influenced by our answers to some of the following questions:

- Would the absence of what I am now doing result in a profound emptiness in my life?
- Will my health and energy level permit me to maintain my present activities in the foreseeable future?
- Will my present standard of living drastically be affected if my salary is replaced by retirement income?
- Are there things I want to do or places I want to see that I could realize and enjoy were it not for what I now am doing?

"Where shall I live?" Shall I stay where I now live, whether it be house, condominium, or apartment? Or shall I consider moving to a retirement center or into the home of another person or family who might have invited me? Again, to help determine our course of action, pondering certain questions is in order:

- Am I content in my present situation?
- Am I physically able to remain where I am?
- Would it be a relief to leave the chores of my present living arrangements to someone else?
- Do I want to attempt to merge into another household and alter the life-style of another person or family as well as my own?
- Could I adjust to living in a community where all would be of my generation?
- Am I willing to surrender some of my freedom in exchange for the security a group-living situation would offer?

Difficult as these choices might be, and although well-meaning family members or friends might feel that they know which answers should be ours, these are choices we must make for ourselves, based on our honest and best judgment at this particular time in our lives!

To Age Need Not Be to Wither!

A common myth about aging is that as we grow older we automatically become less capable and useful. It thus is assumed that as one ages one eventually and necessarily withers into nothingness. How far from the truth is this generalization!

For many people, age is no hindrance. Carl Sandburg wrote *Remembrance Rock* at 70. Benjamin Franklin invented bifocals when he was 78. Sophocles wrote *Oedipus Rex* at 75 and *Oedipus et Colonus* at 89. Titian completed his masterpiece, "The Battle of Lepanto," at 95. And he began work on one of the most famous paintings in the world, "The Descent from the Cross," when he was 97. (Levinson, *Harvard Business Review*, July-August, 1969, p. 52)

There are additional examples. At 100, Grandma Moses still was painting. At 94, Bertrand Russell led international peace drives. At 93, George Bernard Shaw wrote the play *Farfetched Fables*. At 91, Eamon de Valera served as President of Ireland. At 91, Adolph Zukor was chairman of Paramount Pictures. At 90, Pablo Picasso was producing drawings and engravings. At 89, Mary Baker Eddy was directing the Christian Science Church. At 89, Artur Rubinstein gave one of his greatest recitals in New York City's Carnegie Hall. At 89, Albert Schweitzer headed a hospital in Africa. At 88, Pablo Casals was giving cello concerts. At 88, Michelangelo designed the Church of Santa Maria degli Angeli. (*U.S. News and World Report*, September 1, 1980)

To grow older still is to be able to contribute to life!

Life Can Be Beautiful

All of us are growing older. We can fight and rebel unsuccessfully, we can postpone making difficult and perhaps life-changing decisions, or we can accept and adapt to our aging and discover that life can be beautiful, no matter in what stage or state we find ourselves. For, as Harry Levinson once wrote in the *Harvard Business Review* (July-August, 1969, p. 59): "Like wine, people who work over their feelings about the aging process acquire a certain character with age. They deepen their awareness of themselves and others. They see the world in sharper perspective and with greater tolerance. They acquire wisdom. They love more, exploit less. They accept their own imperfection and therefore their own contributions."

God grant that it will be so with each of us!

The Final Chapter

Growing older is accompanied by the distressing phenomenon that we must watch our family members and friends die one by one. This painful reality serves as a reminder that old age brings with it the final chapter in our lives.

We can be dishonest with ourselves and try to deny these experiences that touch our lives with ever-increasing frequency. But to be objective and recognize that none of us will live forever should serve to motivate us to prepare for the time of our own death by making plans with family members or close friends concerning what arrangements we wish to have made at the time of our death. The acceptance of our own mortality should prompt us to have our legal affairs in order. And the knowledge that death one day will come should spur us to share our heartfelt feelings with others—to speak those words of love and to do those acts of love and of kindness while life still is ours!

The deaths of loved ones and friends can have another effect. It can result in what at times will seem to be an overwhelming loneliness. When such is the case ours is the option to yearn for the "good old days" that never can return or to avail ourselves of new groups or situations that will offer the human companionship without which any person is incomplete. I hope we will opt for the latter!

Don't Let Age Be an Excuse!

As some people grow older, they appear to assume that age should be the bestower of benefits and privileges. They act and react as though the passing of years gives them license to be inconsiderate, nasty, and cantankerous. Such people feel that theirs is the inherent right to move to the front of the line, to have doors opened in their path, to have a seat when there is standing room only in public transportation. And if none of the foregoing occurs, their disposition sours!

A danger we confront as we age is that we take for granted such preferential treatment, expecting it rather than being appreciative if and when it occurs. And we can fall into the trap of stereotyping ourselves as reaching a stage in life where we merit being short-tempered rather than patient, dour rather than cheerful, anxious rather than calm, demanding rather than giving, grumpy rather than gracious, set in our ways rather than rolling with the punches.

Let us beware lest we let age be an excuse for being less than the loving and lovable person God and others would have us be!

A Prayer of Gratitude

Eternal God of the ages, to whom years make no difference and whose love is constant throughout life, although there are times when I feel lonely because death is depleting the circle of my family and friends, I am grateful for your abiding presence and for the fact that you never will forsake me. Thank you for all the blessings that have been mine, for the ones you continue to bestow, and for the memories that enrich my life and that nothing can take away! Amen.

The Prayer of an Old Person

In thee, O Lord, do I take refuge; let me never be put to shame! In thy righteousness deliver me and rescue me; incline thy ear to me, and save me! Be thou to me a rock of refuge, a strong fortress, to save me, for thou art my rock and my fortress. . . .

Do not cast me off in the time of old age; forsake me not when my strength is spent. . . .

O God, be not far from me; O my God, make haste to help me! . . . But I will hope continually, and will praise thee yet more and more. My mouth will tell of thy righteous acts, of thy deeds of salvation all the day, for their number is past my knowledge. . . .

O God, from my youth thou hast taught me, and I still proclaim thy wondrous deeds. So even to old age and gray hairs, O God, do not forsake me, till I proclaim thy might to all the generations to come.

—Psalm 71:1–3, 9, 12, 14–15, 17–18

A Prayer for Wisdom

O God, who has been my dwelling place down through the years, how quickly time now passes. The older I become, the shorter each year seems. Therefore, help me to remember that since life will not always be mine, I should do now those things I want to do and say now those words I want to say. Yes, grant me the wisdom to use wisely each day. And may this wisdom brighten my life as well as the lives of those whose paths cross mine! Amen.

God Is Eternal

Lord, thou hast been our dwelling place in all generations. Before the mountains were brought forth, or ever thou hadst formed the earth and the world, from everlasting to everlasting thou art God. . . .

For a thousand years in thy sight are but as yesterday when it is past, or as a watch in the night. . . .

The years of our life are threescore and ten, or even by reason of strength fourscore; yet their span is but toil and trouble; they are soon gone, and we fly away. . . .

So teach us to number our days that we may get a heart of wisdom.

—Psalm 90:1–2, 4, 10, 12

Wisdom Makes the Face Shine

Who is like the wise man? And who knows the interpretation of a thing? A man's wisdom makes his face shine, and the hardness of his countenance is changed. —Ecclesiastes 8:1

A Prayer for Acceptance

O God, the longer I live the more I experience the varied seasons and the cycles of life. There are times of weeping and times of laughing, times of mourning and times of dancing, times of keeping and times of losing, times of birth and times of death. Help me, O Source of Strength, to face life realistically. And during life's dark and difficult experiences, fill me with the hope that brighter hours and days lie ahead. Amen.

Observed the Ancient Preacher:

For everything there is a season, and a time for every matter under heaven:

a time to be born, and a time to die;
a time to plant, and a time to pluck up what is planted;
a time to kill, and a time to heal;
a time to break down, and a time to build up;
a time to weep, and a time to laugh;
a time to mourn, and a time to dance;
a time to cast away stones, and a time to gather stones together;
a time to embrace, and a time to refrain from embracing;
a time to seek, and a time to lose;
a time to keep, and a time to cast away;
a time to rend, and a time to sew;
a time to keep silence, and a time to speak;
a time to love, and a time to hate;
a time for war, and a time for peace.

—Ecclesiastes 3:1–8

A Prayer for Courage

O God, guardian of my life, the older I grow the more frightened I become. I have friends who have been robbed, friends who have fallen and broken bones, friends who are anxious whenever they are alone at home. I am not as strong or surefooted as I was, and at times I feel that I will be unable to cope with an emergency that might confront me.

Grant me the assurance, gracious God, that you are always within me and beside me, and that with the strength of your presence I can withstand whatever comes my way. Amen.

God, Our Strength and Help

The Lord is my light and my salvation; whom shall I fear? The Lord is the stronghold of my life; of whom shall I be afraid? . . . Though a host encamp against me, my heart shall not fear; though war arise against me, yet I will be confident. . . . For he will hide me in his shelter in the day of trouble; he will conceal me under the cover of his tent, he will set me high upon a rock. . . . Hear, O Lord, when I cry aloud, be gracious to me and answer me! . . . Wait for the Lord; be strong, and let your heart take courage; yea, wait for the Lord! —Psalm 27:1, 3, 5, 7, 14

A Prayer When Lonely

O Creator and constant companion, whose presence I feel even when I appear to be alone, I pause to thank you for never leaving or deserting me. You know how keenly I miss those companions and friends from whom I now am separated by death or distance. You know how happy I would be were they beside me right now so I could look into their faces and hear words from their lips.

But how great a store of memories is mine. The experiences we shared are woven into my very being. I therefore know that somehow, O God, with these memories that still are green and with the assurance that you are with me, I can pass through this lonesome valley and will feel happier and more content again. Amen.

Jesus Spoke of God's Presence

If you love me, you will keep my commandments. And I will pray the Father, and he will give you another Counselor, to be with you for ever, even the Spirit of truth, whom the world cannot receive, because it neither sees him nor knows him; you know him, for he dwells with you, and will be in you. I will not leave you desolate; I will come to you. . . . The hour is coming, indeed it has come, when you will be scattered, every man to his home, and will leave me alone; yet I am not alone, for the Father is with me.

—John 14:15–18; 16:32

A Prayer When Health Is Poor

Gracious God, the Great Physician, you know the discouragement and disappointment that are mine because I am in poor health. How much I yearn for the energy that was mine when I was younger. How my heart longs for me to be able to awaken in the morning and be free from aches and pain.

I realize, O God, that you wish that I felt better too. And I realize that I have reached that point in life where my body is no longer that of a teenager. The years have taken their toll. There are problems with which I must learn to live.

Grant me, I pray, the grace to accept and to be able to withstand my discomfort. Enable me to focus on the blessings of the spirit that still are mine. Thank you for my capacity to think, feel, love, and remember. And thank you for what I still am able to do! Amen.

Life Will Not Always Be Easy

For if a man lives many years, let him rejoice in them all; but let him remember that the days of darkness will be many. . . . The years draw nigh, when you will say, "I have no pleasure in them."

—Ecclesiastes 11:8; 12:1

But God Is Always Near

I sought the Lord, and he answered me, and delivered me from all my fears. . . . When the righteous cry for help, the Lord hears, and delivers them out of all their troubles. The Lord is near to the brokenhearted, and saves the crushed in spirit.

—Psalm 34:4, 17–18

"A 17th Century Nun's Prayer"

God, thou knowest better than I know myself that I am growing older and will someday be old. Keep me from the fatal habit of thinking I must say something on every subject and on every occasion.

Release me from craving to straighten out everybody's affairs. Make me thoughtful but not wordy, helpful but not bossy. With my vast store of wisdom, it seems a pity not to use it all, but thou knowest God, that I want a few friends at the end.

Keep my mind free from the recital of endless details; give me wings to get to the point. Seal my lips on my aches and pains. They are increasing, and love of rehearsing them is becoming sweeter as the years go by. I dare not ask for grace enough to enjoy the tales of others' pains, but help me to endure them with patience.

I dare not ask for improved memory, but for a growing humility and a lessening cocksureness when my memory seems to clash with the memories of others. Teach me the glorious lesson that occasionally I may be mistaken.

Keep me reasonably sweet; I do not want to be a saint—some of them are so hard to live with—but a sour old person is one of the crowning works of the devil. Give me the ability to see good things in unexpected places, and talents in unexpected people. And, give me, O God, the grace to tell them so. Amen.

Benedictions

Be, Lord, within me to strengthen me, without me to guard me, over me to shelter me, beneath me to stablish me, before me to guide me, after me to forward me, round about me to secure me. Amen.

—Lancelot Andrewes

May the road rise to meet you.
May the rains fall gently on your fields.
May the wind be always at your back.
May the sun shine warm upon your face.
And, until we meet again,
May God hold you in the palm of his hand. Amen.

—An old Irish prayer

Grow old along with me!
The best is yet to be,
The last of life, for which the first was made:
Our times are in his hand
Who saith, "A whole I planned,
Youth shows but half; trust God:
See all, nor be afraid!"

—Robert Browning